MILK

A Pictorial History of Harvey Milk

MILK

A Pictorial History of Harvey Milk

Introduction and Interview Extracts by
Dustin Lance Black

Foreword by
Armistead Maupin

NEWMARKET PRESS
NEW YORK

Production notes, written by Jason Simos and James Ferrera, courtesy of Focus Features.

First Edition

10 9 8 7 6 5 4 3 2 1   10 9 8 7 6 5 4 3 2 1
ISBN: 978-1-55704-829-5 (hardcover)   ISBN: 978-1-55704-828-8 (paperback)

Library of Congress Catalog-in-Publication Data available upon request.

QUANTITY PURCHASES
Companies, professional groups, clubs, and other organizations may qualify for special terms when ordering
quantities of this title. For information, email sales @newmarketpress.com or write to Special Sales,
Newmarket Press, 18 East 48th Street, New York, NY 10017; call (212) 832-3575 ext. 19 or 1-800-669-3903;
FAX (212) 832-3629. www.newmarketpress.com

Manufactured in the United States of America.

Produced by Newmarket Press: Esther Margolis, Publisher; Frank DeMaio, Production Director;
Keith Hollaman, Editorial Project Director; Paul Sugarman, Digital Supervisor

Designed by Timothy Shaner of Night and Day Design (nightanddaydesign.biz)
Editorial Consultant: Christopher Measom

Other Newmarket Pictorial Moviebooks and Newmarket Insider Film Books include:

The Art of Monsters vs Aliens
The Art of The Matrix*
The Art of X2*
The Art of X-Men: The Last Stand
Bram Stoker's Dracula: The Film and the Legend*
Chicago: The Movie and Lyrics*
Crouching Tiger, Hidden Dragon: A Portrait of
the Ang Lee Film*
Dances with Wolves: The Illustrated Story of the Epic Film*
Dreamgirls : The Movie Musical
E.T. The Extra-Terrestrial: From Concept to Classic*
Gladiator: The Making of the Ridley Scott Epic Film
Good Night, and Good Luck: The Screenplay and
History Behind the Landmark Movie*

Hotel Rwanda: Bringing the True Story of
an African Hero to Film*
The Jaws Log
Memoirs of a Geisha: A Portrait of the Film
The Mummy: Tomb of the Dragon Emperor
The Namesake: A Portrait of the Film by Mira Nair
Ray: A Tribute to the Movie, the Music, and the Man*
Rescue Me: Uncensored
Rush Hour 1, 2, 3: Lights, Camera, Action!
Saving Private Ryan: The Men, The Mission, The Movie
Schindler's List: Images of the Steven Spielberg Film
Superbad: The Illustrated Moviebook*
Tim Burton's Corpse Bride: An Invitation to the Wedding
*Includes screenplay.

www.newmarketpress.com

Contents

HALF-TITLE PAGE: Harvey Milk as a young boy in Woodmere, New York. TITLE PAGE: Candlelight March in memory of Mayor George Moscone and Supervisor Harvey Milk, November 27, 1978.

Armistead Maupin

It's not hard to imagine the joke Harvey Milk might have made about being the subject of an "oral history." He was a bawdy and unembarrassed guy—"sex-positive," as we now so tiresomely call it—so he never missed a chance to send up his own libido; he was part satyr, part Catskill comic, and both instincts energized his political career.

I can't say that I knew Harvey well, but we were brothers in the same revolution. In the late 70s while he was campaigning for supervisor in the Castro, I was across town on Russian Hill cranking out "Tales of the City" for the *San Francisco Chronicle.* Since both efforts were predicated on the then-radical notion that queers deserved a voice in the culture, Harvey and I often found ourselves on the same bill, headlining events that ran the gamut from pride marches to "No on 6" fundraisers to jockstrap auctions at the Stud. We had come of age in a time when homosexuality was not only a mental disease but a criminal offense, so to be oneself and make lemonade from such long-forbidden fruit was exhilarating beyond belief.

Ridiculous as it seems to me now, Harvey and I had both been naval officers and Goldwater Republicans. Like so many gay folks who defected to San Francisco in the early 70s, we'd finally had enough of the shame and secrecy that had stifled our hearts to the point of implosion. Now we were catching up on everything we'd missed, the full fireworks of adolescence: the free-range sex and clumsy puppy love and the simple, giddy freedom of standing-on-the-corner-watching-all-the-boys-go-by.

Harvey was fond of saying that he never considered himself a candidate, that the gay movement itself was the candidate. I'm not sure he believed that *completely*—look at him on the back of that convertible—but it does show how brilliantly he understood the nature of the army he'd assembled. This really *was* about us: the clerk at Macy's, the dyke cop on Valencia, that old tranny singing torch songs in the Tenderloin. It was a movement born of our long frustration and the comforting interconnectedness of *everyone* who had chosen that moment in history to tell the truth; it was born of a love that could finally speak its name.

•

OPPOSITE: (left to right) Daniel Katz, Armistead Maupin, and friend at the launch party for Tales of the City *at the Come Clean Laundromat, San Francisco, August 23, 1978*

Foreword

Let me tell you a story.

In the last month of his life, Harvey Milk met a cute twenty-five-year-old named Steve Beery at the Beaux Arts Ball in San Francisco. Steve was dressed as Robin from the "Batman" comics, so the supervisor introduced himself by tossing out an effectively hokey line—"Hop on my back, Boy Wonder, and I'll fly you to Gotham City." On their first date Harvey asked Steve if he was happy being gay, because Harvey, always on the run, wondered exactly how much on-the-job training would be required. Steve took this to mean that Harvey saw him as serious boyfriend material.

I can't say for sure how many times they got together—half a dozen at the most. On the mornings when Harvey slept over, he would drive Steve to work at a credit union on Geary Boulevard and they would make out in Harvey's Volvo in full view of Steve's co-workers. Sometimes Harvey would call Steve from City Hall and playfully petition for a blow job at his desk. They had made plans to spend Thanksgiving together, but a last-minute crisis at City Hall—reports of the mass suicides at Jonestown—kept Harvey working late again. On another occasion Steve recalled Harvey shrugging off a grisly death threat that had arrived in the mail. "I can't take it seriously," he said. "It was written with a Crayola crayon."

Their last night together was the Friday before Harvey was murdered. Steve remembered it as a night of leisurely cuddling that turned into the gentlest sort of lovemaking. On Monday morning, Steve got the news from a coworker who'd heard it

on the radio. His boss took pity on him and drove him home, where Steve found a note from his roommate saying that Harvey had called that morning with plans for getting together that evening. Numb with disbelief, Steve walked all the way across town to City Hall, where throngs of other people sobbing in the street finally made the tragedy real for him. He didn't try to push his way past the police barricades; he had come into Harvey's life too late to be part of his official history. He had just been in love with the guy.

When Steve worked up the nerve to call Harvey's office, Harvey's aide, Anne Kronenberg, arranged for him to attend the memorial service at the Opera House. "We've been trying to reach you," she told him. "You're one of the chief mourners." Arriving alone at the memorial service, Steve found a seat next to mine and asked if he could take it. He was crying, so for most of the service I held the hand of this stranger. His face was blurry with grief, but I could see what Harvey must have seen: a bright, inquisitive, tender-hearted soul.

For the next fifteen years Steve would be my closest friend, forging a life for himself as an activist and a writer. Like so many of the young men who marched in Harvey's army, he never quite reached middle age, never got to pass on his wisdom. AIDS robs us of more than life; it erases a universe of collective memories and hard-earned experience.

Maybe that's why we're having to learn to kick ass all over again. The generation that knew nothing of Harvey Milk before seeing the movie that bears his name was jolted into a harsh new reality when California voters decided to strip gay people of their right to marry. To us old-timers the argument for Proposition 8 was a blast from the past, a throwback to the evil theocratic Save-the-Children bullshit that Anita Bryant was spewing over thirty years ago. Why, then, was our response so maddeningly weak-kneed and closeted? Why didn't you see images of gay people in any of our ads—or even the *word* "gay," for that matter? Are we that ashamed of ourselves?

The answer is no, thankfully; most of us aren't. And a growing number of young people have lost patience with the black-tie silent-auction-A-gay complacency of the organizations that claim to be fighting for our rights but don't want to ruffle feathers. These new kids are friending each other on Facebook (whatever that means) and taking to the streets on their own. My husband and I met a few of them when we picketed the Mormon temple in Oakland last month. They have love in their eyes and fire in their bellies and a commitment to finish this fight once and for all.

Harvey would have loved them.

—Armistead Maupin
November 2008,
San Francisco

OPPOSITE: Steve Beery, 1981. ABOVE: Harvey Milk campaign buttons.

HARVEY MILK

HARVEY BERNARD MILK

MAY 22, 1930
NOVEMBER 27, 1978

SAN FRANCISCO SUPERVISOR

JANUARY 9 - NOVEMBER 27, 1978

I ASK FOR THE MOVEMENT
TO CONTINUE

Dustin Lance Black

I grew up in a very conservative Mormon military household in San Antonio, Texas. I knew from the age of six what people would call me if they ever discovered my "secret." Faggot. Deviant. Sinner. I'd heard those words ever since I can remember. I knew that I was going to Hell. I was sure God did not love me. It was clear as day that I was "less than" the other kids, and that if anyone ever found out about my little secret, beyond suffering physical harm, I would surely bring great shame to my family.

So I had two choices: to hide—to go on a Mormon mission, to get married and have a small Mormon family (eight to twelve kids)—or to do what I'd thought about many a time while daydreaming in Texas history class: take my own life. Thankfully, there weren't enough pills (fun or otherwise) inside my Mormon mother's medicine cabinet, so I pretended and I hid and I cried myself to sleep more Sabbath nights than I care to remember.

Then, when I was twelve years old, I had a turn of luck. My mom remarried a Catholic Army soldier who had orders to ship out to Fort Ord in Salinas, California. There I discovered a new family, the theater. . . and soon, San Francisco.

That's when it happened. I was almost fourteen when I heard a recording of a speech. It had been delivered on June 9, 1978, the same year my biological father had moved my family out to San Antonio. It was delivered by what I was told was an "out" gay man. His name was Harvey Milk.

> *Somewhere in Des Moines or San Antonio, there is a young gay person who all of a sudden realizes that she or he is gay. Knows that if the parents find out they'll be tossed out of the house. The classmates will taunt the child and the Anita Bryants and John Briggs are doing their bit on TV, and that child has several options: staying in the closet, suicide. . . and then one day that child might*

OPPOSITE: Supervisor Harvey Milk Memorial Sculpture by Daub, Firmin and Hendrickson Sculpture Group, San Francisco City Hall, May 2008

Introduction

open up the paper and it says, "homosexual elected in San Francisco," and there are two new options. One option is to go to California. . . OR stay in San Antonio and fight. You've got to elect gay people so that that young child and the thousands upon thousands like that child know that there's hope for a better world. There's hope for a better tomorrow.

That moment when I heard Harvey for the first time . . . that was the first time I really knew someone loved me for me. From the grave, over a decade after his assassination, Harvey gave me life. . . he gave me hope.

At that very same moment, without knowing it, I became a pawn in a game of political power wrangling that is still shedding blood from DC to Sacramento, El Paso to Altoona. In the following years, I watched careers, political and otherwise, cut short through revelations of this or that official's sexuality. And in 2004, I looked on with horror as a President won re-election by pitting homophobes against gays and lesbians. If there had been a Harvey Milk, if there had been a movement of great hope and change, I certainly couldn't see it from where I stood four and a half years ago when I started this journey to tell Harvey's story.

Thirty years after Harvey Milk was assassinated, in the summer of 2008, with antigay measures on the ballot in several states, I tuned in to the Democratic National Convention to see how his message had fared. Back in 1972, Jim Foster, an openly gay man, stood up in front of the convention and on prime-time national television said, "We do not come to you pleading your understanding or begging your tolerance, we come to you affirming our pride in our life-style, affirming the validity to seek and maintain meaningful emotional relationships and affirming our right to participate in the life of this country on an equal basis with every citizen." What did I hear at the DNC in 2008? Almost nothing. And then there was the Republican National Convention: Sarah Palin, John McCain, flashy, divisive, patriotic speeches. And even there, not a mention of gay or lesbian people. . . bigoted or otherwise.

I left those conventions with a deep, sinking fear. They've found the surefire way to kill the gay and lesbian movement for good. They'll make us invisible. They'll make us all disappear. It's happened before. Reagan did it in the 80s with six years of silence about the AIDS crisis.

OPPOSITE: Harvey Milk at the San Francisco Gay Freedom Day Parade, June 1974

Introduction

You see, one of the biggest hurdles for the gay community has always been invisibility. Unlike the black movement and the women's movement, gays and lesbians are not always immediately identifiable. People still go their entire careers without coming out to their co-workers, not to mention their relatives or their neighbors. Harvey Milk saw this problem, and shouted out the solution, "You must come OUT!"

The entire concept of coming out was devised and pushed for by leaders like Harvey Milk back in 1978 as a way to counter this visibility problem. If people don't know who they are hurting, they don't mind discriminating against them. Watching these two conventions, I got a sinking feeling that Milk's beloved gay and lesbian movement was off the table. I felt myself slowly vanishing, and for gay and lesbian people, invisibility equals death.

Thirty years after Harvey began his fight for GLBT (Gay, Lesbian, Bisexual, Transgender) equality, I am still "less than" a heterosexual when it comes to my civil rights in America. If I fall in love with someone in a foreign country, I can't marry him and bring him home. I can't be out in the military, there are inheritance rights issues, adoption rights, social security, taxation, immigration, employment, housing, and access to health care rights, social services, and education rights, and on and on. The message to gay and lesbian youth today is that they are still inferior.

Today, in 2008, The Gay and Lesbian Task Force reports that a third of all gay youth attempt suicide, that gay youth are four times more likely than straights to try to take their own lives, and if a kid does survive, 26 percent are told to leave home when they come out. It's estimated that 20 to 40 percent of the 1.6 million homeless youth in America today identify as gay or lesbian. Harvey Milk's message is needed now more than ever.

So much of what I've done in this business up to this point has been to make myself ready to take on the overwhelming responsibility of retelling Harvey's story. It took many years of research, digging through archives, driving up to San Francisco in search of Harvey's old friends and foes, charging a couple of nights at the Becks motor lodge on Market and Castro with my principal source, Harvey's political protégé, Cleve Jones.

What I discovered on those trips wasn't the legend of the man that I'd heard in adolescence. What I discovered was a deeply flawed man, a man who had grown up closeted, a man who failed in business and in his relationships, a man who got a very late start. Through Harvey's friends, foes, lovers, and opponents, I met the real Harvey Milk.

Those I interviewed also shared stories of a time in San Francisco when it seemed anything was possible. The Castro was booming. Gay and lesbian people were making headway in the battle for equal rights. And from the ashes of defeats in Florida, Kansas, and Oregon rose a big-eared, floppy-footed leader who was able to reach out to other communities, to the disenfranchised, and to unexpected allies. He convinced an entire people to "come out," and against all odds, he fought back and won on Election Day.

So what happened on Election Day, November 4, 2008, thirty years later? When I began this project, I could never have predicted the parallels between Proposition 8 in California in 2008 and Harvey's fight over Proposition 6 in 1978. Both statewide initiatives sought to take away gay and lesbian rights. By the early hours of November 5, though, it became clear this modern-day fight wouldn't echo Harvey's victory in 1978. Only weeks before Milk's biography would hit the big screen, Proposition 8 in California *passed*. It changed the state's constitution to revoke the right of marriage to gay and lesbian citizens who had already been enjoying that right. Thirty years, almost to the day, after Harvey Milk had successfully defeated Proposition 6 in California, the pendulum had swung back.

One week later, Cleve Jones and I picked up the torch of his former mentor and father figure with these words (as published in the *San Francisco Chronicle*):

We have always been willing to serve our country: in our armed forces, even as we were threatened with courts-martial and dishonor; as teachers, even as we were slandered and libeled; as parents and foster parents struggling to support our children; as doctors and nurses caring for patients in a broken health care system; as artists, writers and musicians; as workers in factories and hotels, on farms and in office buildings; we have always served and loved our country.

We have loved our country even as we have been subjected to discrimination, harassment and violence at the hands of our countrymen. We have loved God, even as we were rejected and abandoned by religious leaders, our churches, synagogues and mosques. We have loved democracy, even as we witnessed the ballot box used to deny us our rights.

We have always kept faith with the American people, our neighbors, co-workers, friends and families. But today that faith is tested and we find ourselves at a crossroad in history.

Will we move forward together? Will we affirm that the American dream is alive and real? Will we finally guarantee full equality under the law for all

Americans? Or will we surrender to the worst, most divisive appeals to bigotry, ignorance and fear?

I imagine Harvey would be surprised that words like these would still be needed in 2008. What went wrong? Why did the GLBT community lose a civil rights fight that Harvey could likely have won thirty years ago?

To me, the answers are clear. GLBT leaders today have been asking straight allies to stand up for the gay community instead of encouraging gay and lesbian people to proudly represent themselves. The movement has become closeted again. The movement has lost the message of Harvey Milk. Who is to blame? The philosopher George Santayana said so long ago, "Those who cannot remember the past are condemned to repeat it."

I didn't grow up with any knowledge of GLBT heroes, but there are many. I didn't grow up with any instruction about GLBT history, but it is a rich history, filled with valuable, universal lessons. It is only in recent years that Hollywood has agreed to risk its dollars on films that depict gay protagonists, and only now, thirty years after Milk's assassination, that Hollywood has agreed to risk its dollars to depict one of the gay movement's greatest heroes.

Now, thanks to the bravery of directors like Gus Van Sant, producers like Dan Jinks and Bruce Cohen, and companies like Michael London's Groundswell and Focus Features, I was given a shot at creating a popularized history that young people, GLBT leaders, and our future straight allies can look at and learn from. With this and the many other films I hope will follow, perhaps we are not doomed to keep repeating the same mistakes of our past.

But even in these difficult times, all is not lost. By example, Harvey taught us that from our darkest hours comes "Hope." The night after this year's election, I attended a rally against the passage of Proposition 8, and the speakers onstage were mostly the folks who had waged the failed, closeted "No on 8" campaign. Yes, they were saying inspiring, fiery words about the injustice. Yes, there were some cheers, but mostly the mood was restless. And then something magical happened.

The young people in the crowd started to move. Perhaps it was instinct, perhaps they knew more about their own movement's history than the folks onstage, perhaps they just weren't willing to continue the current leadership's policy of closeting and good behavior.

OPPOSITE: Harvey Milk at Castro Camera, circa 1974

Introduction

They started to move. They marched away from the stage. They started to march out of the gay ghetto of West Hollywood and up to a straight neighborhood. Within minutes a public march, eight thousand strong, had begun. It looked almost identical to Harvey's marches up Market Street in San Francisco in 1977. Young people, old people, gay people, lesbians, bisexual folks, transgender ones, and many, many straight allies marched up to Sunset Boulevard, took over the city, and started doing what Harvey had talked about. They started giving a face to GLBT people again. They showed the world who was hurt at the ballot box the night before. They came out. They weren't asking straight people to advocate for their rights. In their chants and on their signs, they demanded equality themselves.

In 1977, Harvey Milk claimed Anita Bryant didn't win in Dade County when she overturned all of their gay rights laws. He claimed that the defeat in Florida had brought his people together. It seemed the same thing had happened thirty years later.

And yes, those demonstrators on television, and Harvey's message in theaters, are exceedingly important in the continued fight over Proposition 8, but they are important to me for another, more personal reason. . . because I feel certain there is another kid out there in San Antonio tonight who woke up on November 5, 2008, and heard that gay people had lost their rights in California, that they were still "less than," and I know all too well the dire solutions that may have flashed through his or her head.

Those demonstrators on television sets all across the country aren't just making a statement against the bigotry of Prop 8; they are sending a message of hope to that child in San Antonio: "You are not less than," "You have brothers and sisters and friends, thousands of them," "There is hope for a better tomorrow," and like Harvey said, "You can come to California. . . or you can stay in San Antonio and FIGHT."

These photos and the accompanying quotes from my research interviews in this book don't tell the story of a man born to lead, but of a regular man with many flaws who did what many others wouldn't . . . he did what his people need to do again today, thirty years later . . . Harvey Milk stood up and fought back.

—Dustin Lance Black
November 2008,
Los Angeles

OPPOSITE: Supervisor Harvey Milk as Deputy Mayor for a day, March 7, 1978

East Coast Life (Pre-1972)

Harvey Bernard Milk was born on May 22, 1930, in Woodmere, New York. He had one brother. He graduated in 1951 from New York State Teachers College at Albany. He joined the Navy, serving as chief petty officer on a submarine rescue ship, and was discharged in 1955. First he taught high school, then in 1963 went to work on Wall Street for Bache and Company. During the late 60s he began dabbling in off-Broadway theater production and moved to San Francisco with his then lover, Jack McKinley, who was working on the San Francisco production of the musical *Hair*. Harvey worked in finance until he publicly burned his BankAmericard and was fired from his job. He returned to New York in 1970, where he met Scott Smith. Two years later, with Scott by his side, he decided to give San Francisco another go.

1947

Harvey Milk
"Glimpy"

And they say WOMEN are never at a loss for words!

MILK, Harvey. Football 3, 4; Basketball 3, 4; Variety Show; Jr. Prom Committee.

Harvey was a popular student, a basketball player, and a linebacker on the football team at Bay Shore High School. His big ears, feet, and nose earned him the nickname Glimpy. Although no one ever would have guessed he was "a sissy," his yearbook photo was tagged with "Glimpy Milk—And they say WOMEN are never at a loss for words."

OPPOSITE: Harvey Milk as a young boy in Woodmere, New York. TOP: Young Harvey (left) and his brother Robert, Coney Island, New York, September 1, 1942. ABOVE: Harvey Milk's 1947 yearbook entry from Bay Shore High School, Bay Shore, New York.

Milk joined the Navy three months after graduating high school. He rose quickly through the ranks to be chief petty officer of the U.S.S. *Kittiwake*, a San Diego–based aircraft carrier that cruised the Pacific. After three years and eleven months he was honorably discharged.

OPPOSITE: *Harvey Milk in navy dress whites, circa 1955. ABOVE: Sailor Harvey Milk (right) and companion, circa mid-1950s. BELOW: Harvey Milk (second from left, standing) and friends shortly after his discharge from the military in Los Angeles, California, where he resided briefly, circa 1955.*

He was in the Navy. He was a stockbroker. He loved opera. He was a Republican. He campaigned for Goldwater. And then while he was still in New York, he met Tom O'Horgan, the director of *Hair* and *Lenny*. He quit his job, and became sort of a hippie. He was a little old to be a hippie but he grew his hair. He fell in love with Scott Smith, got into some kinky sex, and moved to San Francisco.

—*Cleve Jones*

OPPOSITE: Harvey Milk outside the Brooks Atkinson Theatre, New York City, after picking up tickets for the Broadway play Lenny, *1972*

The Castro: 1972

Abutting the slopes of Twin Peaks just in the center of San Francisco is the neighborhood now known as the Castro—six square blocks about two miles west of City Hall that is named after its main thoroughfare. Castro Street, in turn, was named for José Castro, the governor of Alta California who acquired the land (then called Rancho San Justo) from the Mexican government during the secularization of Mission lands in the 1830s. A half century later the Market Street Cable Railway Company extended its line from downtown

Harvey spent most of his life looking for a stage. On Castro Street, he finally found it.
—Tom O'Horgan

to the area and a neighborhood was born. Many Swedish, Norwegian, and Finnish homesteaders followed the tracks out to the valley, and from 1910 to 1920 the neighborhood was known as "little Scandinavia." By the 1930s, it was overwhelmingly an Irish working-class neighborhood called Eureka Valley, filled with kids—the art deco Castro Theater acting as babysitter many a Saturday and Sunday afternoon—and thriving businesses.

In the 1960s, crime, drugs, and the growing hippie movement drove many families to the suburbs, leaving their cute-but-fading Victorian houses behind. The "hippies"—who were mainly middle-class, well-educated young people from all across the United States—lent San Francisco an air of freedom, counter-culture, and sexual revolution that attracted gays and lesbians (among other disenfranchised people). Beside seeking freedom they were also in search of cheap rent and found it in Eureka Valley. By 1977 20,000 gay

LEFT: Elderly resident at the corner of 18th and Castro watching the pageantry of the Third Annual Castro Street Fair, August 1976. OPPOSITE: Revelry at the Gay Freedom Day Celebration in Marks Meadows, Golden Gate Park, San Francisco, June 1975. FOLLOWING PAGES: Third Annual Castro Street Fair, August 1976.

people had moved into the neighborhood and brought their culture with them—street fairs, freedom parades, Halloween extravaganzas, gay newspapers, softball leagues, choirs, and even a tap-dancing troupe.

Needless to say, tensions increased. Cleve Jones, who lived through this transition, commented, "As we began moving over the hill from the Haight-Ashbury into the Castro, playgrounds became cruisy at night. For a neighborhood that had recently been Irish Catholic to suddenly be full of half naked men smoking pot all over the place at 4 a.m. was very jarring for them."

Violence and harassment—even from the police—became part of the mix on Castro Street. But with economic power, and the strength of being in a supportive community for the first time, came a push for political power.

As the 21st century dawns, the Castro—while still unmistakably gay—is not quite the Mecca it once was. The area has gentrified, and the expensive real estate excludes many. At the same time cultural acceptance of gay, lesbian, bisexual, and transgender people (born of the power and visibility that sprang from this neighborhood) has grown massively since Harvey's time, allowing gay people more choice about living openly and safely in more cities and neighborhoods than ever. Today the neighborhood is more a gayish gift-shop Mecca or, as Armistead Maupin recently (and affectionately) called it, "Gayberry."

We were trying to build a ghetto. It gave us power and a cultural caldron out of which came so much. The first gay synagogue, the first gay games, the first rainbow flag, and all of these things we take for granted now.
—*Cleve Jones*

OPPOSITE: *Harmodius and Hoti at the Second Annual Castro Street Fair, August 1975.* ABOVE: *Tony Angel from the free theater group* The Angels of Light *at the Second Annual Castro Street Fair, August 1975. Following pages: San Francisco Gay Freedom Day Celebration.*

Castro Camera

After having a roll of film ruined at a local pharmacy, Harvey and Scott used their last bit of savings (mostly from unemployment checks) to buy up camera supplies, sign a five-year lease on a Castro Street Victorian storefront, and open "Castro Camera." In March of 1973, they hung a sign in the window that announced, "We are VERY open."

My oldest daughter was twelve at the time and just about to graduate from Grattan elementary school. We had taken pictures at the graduation and I brought them down to Harvey's camera store on Castro Street. It was my first time ever meeting him. I brought the film in and went back a couple of days later to pick it up. I brought it home and with all the kids and my grandmother sitting around the table, I took out the pictures . . . and it was all naked men!

I brought the film back to Harvey and I said—I didn't even know who he was really—I said, "I think I've got the wrong film." He looked at the pictures and said, "Yes, I think you have," and we both started laughing. From that moment on, I was just endeared to him.

—*Sharon Johnson, Castro Camera patron*

OPPOSITE: Voter registration table in front of Castro Camera during the First Annual Castro Street Fair, August 1974. Photo © Rink Foto 1978. RIGHT: Rich Nichols and Harvey Milk in front of Larry Piet's Valentine's Day installation at Castro Camera, February 1977.

ABOVE: Harvey Milk at Castro Camera, circa mid-1970s. BELOW: Dan Nicoletta working at Castro Camera, circa mid-1970s. OPPOSITE: David Waggoner helping out at Castro Camera, winter 1977.

Political Hangout

I met Harvey because I used to take a lot of photographs, and he ran the camera shop. He had the barber chair there and we would just talk and chat about Castro Street.

—*Walter Park, former Castro resident*

I was going to City College. They had a really good film faculty, so I would go into Castro Camera from time to time. I really liked this guy Danny, this boy that worked with Harvey and Scott. I just started hanging out at the camera store.

It was sort of a drop-in center where Harvey would help you. If you needed to figure out how to get your kid into a specialty program for the mentally disabled, he'd figure out a way to do it. If you were a drag queen and wanted to do a benefit for the youth center, he'd help you. He was just always helping people, fixing problems, like getting a stop sign put in on the corner of a dangerous intersection, that kind of thing.

—*Cleve Jones*

TOP: Harvey Milk and Scott Smith at Castro Camera, circa mid-1970s. LEFT: Scott Smith getting two cream pies in his face on his birthday, October 21, 1975. OPPOSITE: Scott Smith selling film at the San Francisco Gay Freedom Day Parade, circa 1974.

Boycott & Early Gay Allies

The Teamsters launched a boycott in response to Coors' anti-union stance. There was a lot of racism in the company and, of course, they wouldn't hire gay people. But the Coors boycott was so important because Harvey met this very straight, older Teamster organizer named Allan Baird and Harvey saw this opportunity—which was one of his most significant contributions—to form a gay-labor alliance. Allan and Harvey became fast friends. This was Harvey's gift, his ability to befriend and create genuine relationships. He was all about connecting, whether it was reaching out to an old Irish widow who didn't like the gay boys smoking pot on her stairs or to a macho truckers' union. But beyond that, those of us from the left who were more political got to see the gay struggle as being part of a larger struggle for peace and social justice around the world.

—Cleve Jones

The tradeoff was, "I'll make sure that Coors beer isn't sold in any gay bars, but I hope you will increase the number of gay truck drivers, gay delivery men." It worked! The Teamsters supported Harvey.

—Jim Rivaldo

TOP: Teamster leader Allan Baird onstage with Harvey Milk at the second supervisorial election campaign party at the Island Restaurant, 1976. LEFT: Gay revolution flag with the Castro Theatre in the background. OPPOSITE: Coors Boycott poster and button re-created for the movie Milk.

44

BOYCOTT

WORKER HARRASSMENT
CONSUMER ABUSE
UNION BUSTING
RACISM

¡BASTA YA!
RACISMO
PERSECUION AL OBRERO
ABUSO AL CONSUMIDOR
ROMPIMIENTO DE LA UNIÓN

COORS BEER

204 ... HOWARD QUINN CO.

The Players

Scott Smith

Known affectionately to friends as "the widow Milk," Scott Smith was born in Key West, Florida, to a Navy couple who raised him in Jackson, Mississippi. He moved to New York in 1969, where he met and fell in love with Harvey Milk. Their relationship lasted seven years. In 1972 they moved to San Francisco and opened Castro Camera. After Harvey's assassination Scott fought for and was awarded $5,500 in survivor's death benefits by the San Francisco retirement board. He died of AIDS-related pneumonia at age 46 shortly after attending the premiere of the opera *Harvey Milk.*

For a lot of straight people, he was the first nonstereotypical gay person they had ever met. Harvey was just like everybody else. With his humor and his caring for people, he made people like him. — *Scott Smith*

I first met Scott Smith in late 1973 after Harvey Milk and Scott moved to Castro Street. Scott introduced my wife and me to Harvey. Scott was full of pride as he talked about Harvey, who was taking his first shot at running for public office in San Francisco. From that day on, Scott stayed in the shadow of Harvey, who was his lover and partner in a camera shop business.

I told Scott and Harvey what it was like to grow up in the Castro District in the 1930s. It became clear that Scott and Harvey's main interest was to make our community a better place for all, whether gay or straight.

As a young Teamster official in 1973, I made a decision to speak out for gay rights and endorse and support Harvey for public office. Harvey Milk became the first openly gay person to be elected Supervisor of San Francisco.

There is an old saying that behind every successful man there is a woman. In Harvey's case, it was a man: Scott Smith. In 1974, I was directing the boycott of Coors beer. Harvey was the name out in front, but Scott was in the shadow giving me help and advice. My wife and I continued to be friends of Scott over the next 20 years.

We always respected Scott for the love of his mother. He phoned his mom every Sunday and talked for one hour. She lived in Mississippi.

Scott phoned me in December 1994 and said, "Allan, we are invited to the premiere of the Harvey Milk opera in Houston, Texas." Due to illness in my family, I had to decline. I met with Scott when he returned. He was full of pride and joy.

I said, "Scott, you've finally come out of the shadow of Harvey. You are now getting the recognition you deserve."

I'm so glad that Scott could see the opera before his death. He was also looking forward to the movie *Harvey Milk*, whenever it will come to the big screen.

I met Scott on Castro Street the day before he went into the hospital. He said, "I feel fine." He died on February 4.

I asked him how his mom was, and Scott said, "She's great. But if she ever needs me, I will have her with me and care for her." Scott was a dedicated son.

A host of Scott's loving friends joined his mother to take Scott's ashes out to sea on February 11 in the bright light of day. No more shadows for Scott.

—*Allan Baird, retired President of Teamsters Local 921, San Francisco*

OPPOSITE: Scott Smith and Harvey Milk at Castro Camera, circa 1974. RIGHT: Scott Smith in New York City subway, circa early 1970s.

Cleve Jones, founder of The

NAMES Project AIDS Memorial Quilt, was born
in West Lafayette, Indiana, in 1954.

Cleve's career as an activist began in San
Francisco during the turbulent 1970s, when he was
befriended by Harvey Milk. After Milk's election
Cleve worked in the office as a student intern while
studying political science at San Francisco State
University. After Harvey's death Cleve dropped out
of school and worked in Sacramento as a legislative
consultant to California State Assembly Speakers
Leo T. McCarthy and Willie L. Brown, Jr.

In 1982 he returned to San Francisco to work
in the district office of State Assemblyman Art
Agnos. Cleve was elected to three terms on the San
Francisco Democratic County Central Committee,

and served on local and state commissions for
juvenile justice and delinquency prevention and
the Mission Mental Health Community Advisory
Board.

Recognizing the threat of AIDS, Cleve co-
founded the San Francisco AIDS Foundation in
1983. He conceived the idea of the AIDS Memorial
Quilt at a candlelight memorial for Harvey Milk in
1985; he created the first quilt panel in honor of his
close friend Marvin Feldman in 1987. Since then,
the NAMES Project AIDS Memorial Quilt has
grown to become the world's largest community

*ABOVE: Sally Gearhart and Cleve Jones at Castro
Street rally on Harvey's birthday, the night after the
White Night Riots, May 22, 1979. OPPOSITE: Dan
Nicoletta at Castro Camera, 1976.*

The first time I met him was at the corner of Castro and 18th. He was passing out flyers. And he was flirty, like "You look good, I like the way your pants fit." But not at all in a way that was creepy. —*Cleve Jones*

arts project, memorializing the lives of over 85,000 Americans killed by AIDS.

Cleve has served as a member of the International Advisory Board of the Harvard AIDS Institute; the National Board of Governors of Project Inform; and the Board of Directors of the Foundation for AIDS and Immune Research.

As a public speaker, he travels extensively throughout the United States and around the world, lecturing at high schools, colleges, and universities.

Cleve Jones currently resides in Palm Springs, California; he works as a community organizer for the Hotel Workers Rising campaign of UNITE HERE, the international union representing textile, hotel, and restaurant workers.

His best-selling memoir, *Stitching a Revolution*, was published in April 2000.

Danny Nicoletta

Native New Yorker Danny Nicoletta is a San Francisco-based freelance photographer who began his career in the city in 1975 as an assistant to the late Crawford Barton, who was then the staff photographer for *The Advocate*.

During this time, he also worked in Harvey Milk and Scott Smith's camera store in the heart of San Francisco's Castro District. Danny basically ran the store himself and assisted in several of Milk's political campaigns.

Since 1989, he has concentrated his photography on studio portraits of the souls who populate the lesbian, gay, bisexual, and transgender (LGBT) community, while continuing to document the journey of the LGBT civil rights movement. He had a featured exhibition at Mace Gallery, as well as a one man retrospective at the corporate headquarters of Levi Strauss & Company in San Francisco. His photography has been collected by the Wallach Collection of Fine Prints; the Berg Collection at the New York Public Library; the James C. Hormel Gay and Lesbian Center at the San Francisco Public Library; the Schwules Museum in Berlin; and by private archivists.

Danny has continued to further Harvey's legacy in the decades since, making his photographic archives available for research and reference.

I'd always been involved in political movements, the women's movement, the environment. When I was 15 I opened up the first environmental recycling center in my town, Bellevue, Washington. When I came to San Francisco I became involved in the lesbian movement. Harvey called me his little dykette. I got so much from Harvey it's hard to think that I offered him anything. Loyalty, dedication, a willingness to just soak it all in, I suppose. I was a sponge.

—Anne Kronenberg

Anne Kronenberg

began her long career in government service as an aide to Supervisor Harvey Milk after having been campaign manager for his historic election to the San Francisco Board of Supervisors.

Anne was appointed to the State Board of Podiatric Medicine in 1998, serving as the President of the Board for three years and Vice President for two. Prior to her tenure with the Department of Public Health, she was Director of the San Francisco Mayor's Criminal Justice Council from 1991-1994.

She co-chaired the San Francisco Local Homeless Coordinating Board for three years, and has chaired the San Francisco Board of Supervisors' Single Room Occupancy Task Force since its inception in 1998.

Anne has extensive government experience, having worked at the federal level for Senator Ted Kennedy; at the state level for Assemblyman John Vasconcellos; and at the local level on both the legislative and executive sides of government.

She is currently Deputy Director for Administration and Planning of the San Francisco Department of Public Health, where she has worked—serving in a number of previous capacities including Director of External Affairs, Public Information Officer, and Government Relations—for nearly 15 years.

Jim Rivaldo

"I majored in government at Harvard and figured I'd go into politics. But then as I realized I was gay, I thought that that whole avenue was closed off to me and I had to come up with something else. But through Harvey—seeing how positive people responded to him—I realized that I could be gay and still work in politics. He was my personal therapy. I helped him and he helped me.

"I ended up writing and designing his political propaganda; his brochures, his themes. He would write a rough draft of what he wanted to say and I would clean it up. For such an articulate guy, some of his stuff was just unintelligible." *—Jim Rivaldo*

OPPOSITE: (left to right) Dick Pabich, Anne Kronenberg, and Jim Rivaldo, Election Day at Castro Camera, November 8, 1977

Michael Wong met Harvey

Milk in 1973 at a candidates' night event. At the time, Michael was active in the SF Young Democrats, United Black Education Caucus, and Chinese American Democratic Club. It was in the Fred Harris for President campaign that Harvey won over many of his "straight" volunteers and friends, including Mr. Wong. As a result, Michael became an advisor for Harvey's 1975 campaign for Supervisor and the 1976 State Assembly race, where the two became good friends. Milk soon began affectionately referring to Michael as "Lotus Blossom." Michael retired from politics for a time after Bill Clinton won election in 1996, only to be pulled back into the political scene by the Barack Obama campaign in 2008.

"Dick Pabich walked into the

1976 campaign licking his wounds from a failed relationship, wanting something to do. He was 20, tall, arrogant, had sort of a command presence and was known for throwing big parties back in Wisconsin. He had a curly bleach blond hairdo and he sort of was of the David Bowie era aesthetically.

When Harvey died, Dick left City Hall. He was with Harry Britt for just a little while and then he and I opened up a political consultancy office on Castro Street." —Jim Rivaldo

I thought he was a nut. At the time Texas had somebody killing a lot of men, it was Texas homosexual murders. (Harvey) thought that he could get publicity 'cause he was openly gay and (the murderer) might shoot him at a candidate night thing. —*Mike Wong*

ABOVE: Jim Rivaldo (left) and Dick Pabich, Election Day at Castro Camera, November 8, 1977. OPPOSITE: Supervisor Harvey Milk and Michael Wong, March 7, 1978.

1st Run . . . 1st Loss

Masturbation can be fun but it does not take the place of the real thing. It is about time that the gay community stopped playing with itself and got down to the real thing. There are people who are satisfied with crumbs because that is all they think they can get, when in reality, if they demand the real thing, they will find that they indeed can get it.

— *Harvey Milk on his first run for public office*

We don't want to be harassed. And also we want the equal opportunity for work. I pay my taxes, but I'm not allowed to be a policeman— Oh, they say you are allowed, but you aren't. I'm not allowed to be a fireman. And if I have to pay my taxes, why shouldn't I have civil rights?

—*Harvey Milk*

OPPOSITE and ABOVE: Harvey Milk campaigning on Castro Street, circa 1973.

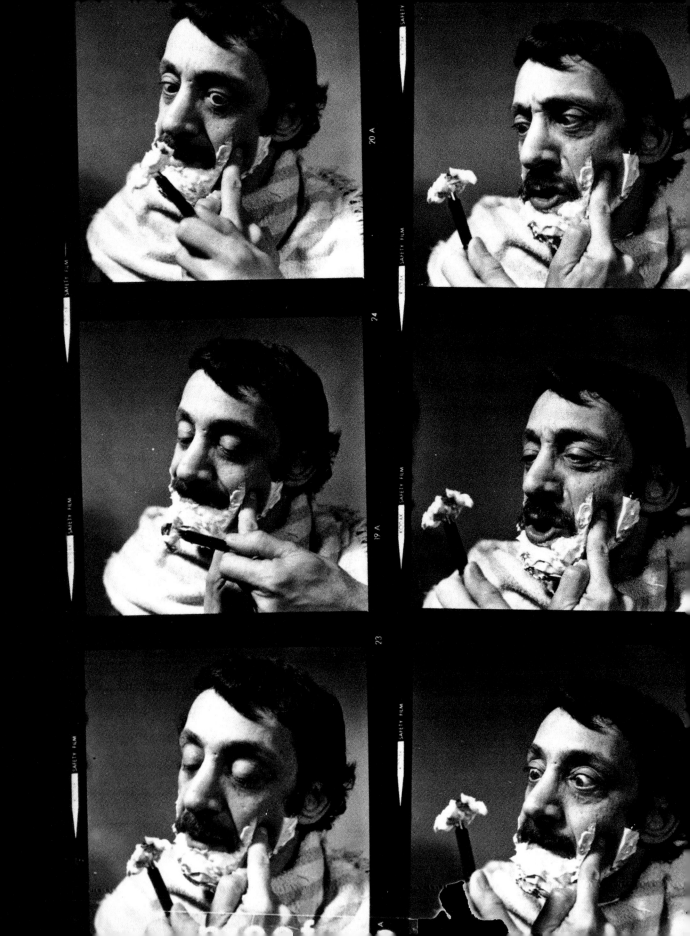

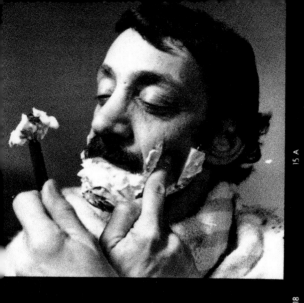

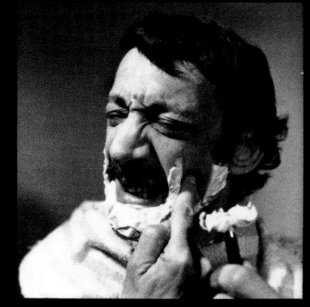

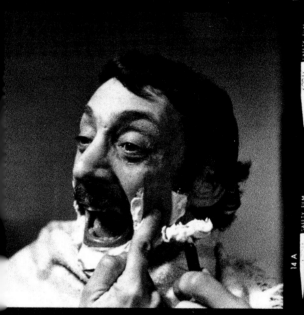

At a fund-raiser a man approached me and gave me a warm smile. It was Harvey Milk, the long-haired hippie candidate for Supervisor. Only now he had short hair and he was clean-shaven. He was also wearing a suit. I was surprised. "Hi, Mike, like the new look?" I told him I was floored. "Well, you have to make compromises in order to win elections. I'm running for Supervisor next year and would love to get your support."

—Mike Wong

Harvey Milk posing for a student photography project, circa mid-1970s.

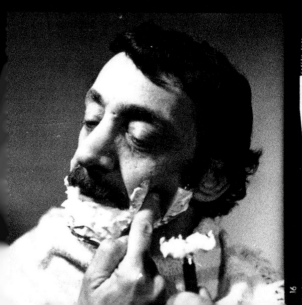

2nd Run . . . 2nd Loss

When he cut his mustache off he said, "I want no distractions. Fifty people may not like mustaches, and I'm not gonna lose by 50 votes.". . . He didn't have a suit but he used to pick up leftover laundry from the dry cleaners up on the corner. You know, the clothing that had been there for months, he went and picked it up. They gave the suit to him. —*Jim Rivaldo*

OPPOSITE: (left to right) Doug Perry, Harvey Milk, Eric Garber, and Cleve Jones at Cleve Jones's twenty-fourth birthday party at the Elephant Walk Bar on Castro Street, October 11, 1978. Photo © Rink Foto 1978. ABOVE: Milk campaign volunteer Medora Payne (right) and her mom, Gretchen Payne, camping it up with Harvey at Castro Camera, February 1977.

3rd Run . . .
3rd Loss

The mayor appointed him to the Board of Permit Appeals by promising not to run against the traditionalist people who were getting ready to run their candidate, Art Agnos. Harvey immediately turned around and announced his candidacy and the mayor fired him, thus getting front-page headlines all over the place. And then Harvey was seen even more as this independent, iconoclastic, crazy hippie bad boy. —*Cleve Jones*

We were debating at Hastings College of Law and I kinda liked him. And I said, "Harvey, you know you really gotta change your rap, it's a downer." He had this kind of rap like, "throw the bums out," I called it. And what he would do is accuse me of being a lifelong government bureaucrat type who only wanted to give social programs out to people and didn't understand the taxpayer. He was still in that sort of Republican conservative mode. I said, "You know, that really doesn't work with this city, you've really gotta give people a reason for optimism. You've gotta make them think about the future in a positive way." That guy was so quick, like that it clicked. I'll be damned if the next time we were together he had that Hope speech. I remember him talking about the kid from Altoona that he wanted to give hope to. I'd never heard this before. He just shifted. —*Art Agnos*

ABOVE: Harvey Milk campaigning at a music concert in Golden Gate Park, San Francisco, circa 1977.

Orange Tuesday
June 7, 1977

MIAMI, May 9—A dispute over rights for homosexuals, building locally for the last several months, is focusing attention on a national issue.

As far as the Miami area is concerned the argument will be settled on June 7, when residents vote to repeal or uphold a county ordinance that bars discrimination against homosexuals in employment, housing and public accommodations.

But both sides in the fight have vowed to continue the struggle elsewhere in the country, whatever the outcome of the Miami referendum. National committees are being organized and fund drives are under way in "gay" bars and fundamentalist churches from here to San Francisco. . . .

. . . The main figure in the dispute is Anita Bryant, the Miami television singer known nationwide for her sunny purveying of Florida orange juice and her devoutly patriotic rendering of "The Battle Hymn of the Republic." A fervent Southern Baptist, the 37-year-old mother of four school-age children heads Save Our Children Inc., the main anti-homosexual group.

"If homosexuality were the normal way, God would have made Adam and Bruce," she says.

— *B. Drummond Ayres, Jr., excerpted from* The New York Times, *May 10, 1977*

OPPOSITE: Harvey Milk in San Francisco protesting against the repeal of gay rights in Dade County, Florida, Orange Tuesday, June 7, 1977. ABOVE: San Francisco Gay and Lesbian Freedom Day Parade contingent equating anti-gay crusader Anita Bryant with fascists, June 1977. Photos © by Jerry Pritikin.

Harvey Runs Again

Harvey felt that nobody gives you your rights, you have to go out and get them yourself and sometimes you need to ruffle some feathers and push too hard and bruise some people's sensitivities . . . you gotta be aggressive and sacrifice some of your social acceptance to promote what's really important to you, which was gay rights. —*Jim Rivaldo*

OPPOSITE and ABOVE: Harvey Milk at Castro Camera, circa 1977.

Anne Kronenberg came into the office and was sort of peppy and young and politically naïve, but very committed . . . plus, at the time, she was a lesbian.

—*Jim Rivaldo*

I knew the camera shop because that's where I developed my film, but I didn't know Harvey. He was an icon, so I never talked to him. But a friend of mine sent Harvey a fifty-dollar campaign contribution along with a note saying he should talk to me because "she's young and smart and maybe there's some kind of connection there." And so out of the blue Harvey called me to talk about a job. I was doing secretarial work at a company I just hated at the time and he said, "Do you want to do the campaign?" and I said, "yes." So he said, "I can't pay you but we'll figure out some way to make your rent." I quit my job and went to work for him as campaign coordinator. I knew nothing.

—*Anne Kronenberg*

ABOVE: (left to right) Jim Rivaldo, Lee, Anne Kronenberg, Dick Pabich, and Harvey Milk on Election Day at Castro Camera, November 8, 1977. OPPOSITE: Denton Smith and Harvey Milk at Castro Camera, 1976. FOLLOWING PAGES: Harvey forces a meeting with Jimmy Carter at a "Carter for President" campaign stop, San Francisco, 1976.

ABOVE: Enthusiastic students visiting Harvey Milk's camera store/political campaign headquarters on Election Day, November 8, 1977. OPPOSITE: Harvey Milk leafleting the Fourth Annual Castro Street Fair, August 1977. Photo © Rink Foto 1978.

The Hope Speech

My name is Harvey Milk and I'm here to recruit you.

I've been saving this one for years. It's a political joke. I can't help it—I've got to tell it. I've never been able to talk to this many political people before, so if I tell you nothing else you may be able to go home laughing a bit.

This ocean liner was going across the ocean and it sank. And there was one little piece of wood floating and three people swam to it and they realized only one person could hold on to it. So they had a little debate about which was the person. It so happened the three people were the Pope, the President, and Mayor Daley. The Pope said he was titular head of one of the great religions of the world and he was spiritual adviser to many, many millions and he went on and pontificated and they thought it was a good argument. Then the President said he was leader of the largest and most powerful nation of the world. What takes place in this country affects the whole world and they thought that was a good argument. And Mayor Daley said he was mayor of the backbone of the United States and what took place in Chicago affected the world, and what took place in the archdiocese of Chicago affected Catholicism. And they thought that was a good argument. So they did it the democratic way and voted. And Daley won, seven to two.

About six months ago, Anita Bryant in her speaking to God said that the drought in California was because of the gay people. On November 9, the day after I got elected, it started to rain. On the day I got sworn in, we walked to City Hall and it was

kinda nice, and as soon as I said the words "I do," it started to rain again. It's been raining since then and the people of San Francisco figure the only way to stop it is to do a recall petition. That's a local joke.

So much for that. Why are we here? Why are gay people here? And what's happening? What's happening to me is the antithesis of what you read about in the papers and what you hear about on the radio. You hear about and read about this movement to the right. That we must band together and fight back this movement to the right. And I'm here to go ahead and say that what you hear and read is what they want you to think because it's not

ABOVE: (left to right) Harvey Milk, Frank Robinson (Harvey's speechwriter who helped write the Hope Speech), and Tom O'Horgan at Castro Camera, 1974-75.

happening. The major media in this country had talked about the movement to the right so much that they've got even us thinking that way. Because they want the legislators to think that there is indeed a movement to the right and that the Congress and the legislators and the city councils will start to move to the right the way the major media want them. So they keep on talking about this move to the right.

So let's look at 1977 and see if there was indeed a move to the right. In 1977, gay people had their rights taken away from them in Miami. But you must remember that in the week before Miami and the week after that, the word *homosexual* or *gay* appeared in every single newspaper in this nation in articles both pro and con. In every radio station, in every TV station and every household. For the first time in the history of the world, everybody was talking about it, good or bad. Unless you have dialogue, unless you open the walls of dialogue, you can never reach to change people's opinion. In those two weeks, more good and bad, but *more* about the words *homosexual* and *gay* was written than probably in the history of mankind. Once you have dialogue starting, you know you can break down the prejudice. In 1977 we saw a dialogue start. In 1977, we saw a gay person elected in San Francisco. In 1977 we saw the state of Mississippi decriminalize marijuana. In 1977, we saw the convention of conventions in Houston. And I want to know where the movement to the right is happening.

What that is is a record of what happened last year. What we must do is make sure that 1978 continues the movement that is really happening that the media don't want you to know about, that is the movement to the left. It's up to CDC to put the pressures on Sacramento—not to just bring flowers to Sacramento—but to break down the walls and the barriers so the movement to the left continues and progress continues in the nation. We have before us coming up several issues we must speak out on. Probably the most important issue outside the Briggs—which we will come to—but we do know what will take place this June. We know there's an issue on the ballot called Jarvis-Gann. We hear the taxpayers talk about it on both sides. But what you don't hear is that it's probably the most racist issue on the ballot in a long time. In the city and county of San Francisco, if it passes and we indeed have to lay off people, who will they be? The last in, not the first in, and who are the last in but the minorities? Jarvis-Gann is a racist issue. We must address that issue. We must not talk away from it. We must not allow them to talk about the money it's going to save, because look at who's going to save the money and who's going to get hurt.

We also have another issue that we've started in some of the north counties and I hope in some of the south counties it continues. In San Francisco elections we're asking—at least we hope to ask—that the U.S. government put pressure on the closing of the South African consulate. That must happen. There is a major difference between an embassy in Washington, which is a diplomatic bureau, and a consulate in major cities. A consulate is there for one reason only—to promote business, economic gains, tourism, investment. And every time you have business going to South Africa, you're promoting a regime that's offensive.

In the city of San Francisco, if everyone of 51 percent of that city were to go to South Africa, they would be treated as second-class citizens. That is an offense to the people of San Francisco and I hope all my colleagues up there will take every step we can to close down that consulate and hope that people in other parts of the state follow us in that lead. The battles must be started someplace, and CDC is the greatest place to start the battles.

I know we are pressed for time so I'm going to cover just one more little point. That is to understand why it is important that gay people run for office and that gay people get elected. I know there are many people in this room who are running for central committee who are gay. I encourage you. There's a major reason why. If my non-gay friends and supporters in this room understand it, they'll probably understand why I've run so often before I finally made it. Y'see right now, there's a controversy going on in the convention about the governor. Is the speaking out enough? Is he strong enough for gay rights? And there is a controversy and for us to say it is not would be foolish. Some people are satisfied and some people are not.

You see there is a major difference—and it remains a vital difference—between a friend and a gay person, a friend in office and a gay person in office. Gay people have been slandered nationwide. We've been tarred and we've been bruised with the picture of pornography. In Dade County, we were accused of child molestation. It's not enough anymore just to have friends represent us. No matter how good that friend may be.

The black community made up its mind to that a long time ago. That the myths against blacks can only be dispelled by electing black leaders, so the black community could be judged by the leaders and not by the myths or black criminals. The Spanish community must not be judged by Latin criminals or myths. The Asian community must not be judged by Asian criminals or myths. The Italian community should not be judged by the mafia myths. And the time has come when the gay community must not be judged by our criminals and myths.

Like every other group, we must be judged by our leaders and by those who are themselves gay, those who are visible. For invisible, we remain in limbo—a myth, a person with no parents, no brothers, no sisters, no friends who are straight, no important positions in employment. A tenth of a nation supposedly composed of stereotypes and would-be seducers of children—and no offense meant to the stereotypes. But today, the black community is not judged by its friends, but by its black legislators and leaders. And we must give people the chance to judge us by our leaders and legislators. A gay person in office can set a tone, can command respect not only from the larger community, but from the young people in our own community who need both examples and hope.

The first gay people we elect must be strong. They must not be content to sit in the back of the bus. They must not be content to accept pablum. They must be above wheeling and dealing. They must be—for the good of all of us—independent,

OPPOSITE: Supervisor Harvey Milk at his inauguration dinner, January 10, 1978

unbought. The anger and the frustration that some of us feel is because we are misunderstood, and friends can't feel that anger and frustration. They can sense it in us, but they can't feel it. Because a friend has never gone through what is known as coming out. I will never forget what it was like coming out and having nobody to look up toward. I remember the lack of hope—and our friends can't fulfill that.

I can't forget the looks on faces of people who've lost hope. Be they gay, be they seniors, be they blacks looking for an almost-impossible job, be they Latins trying to explain their problems and aspirations in a tongue that's foreign to them. I personally will never forget that people are more important than buildings. I use the word "I" because I'm proud. I stand here tonight in front of my gay sisters, brothers, and friends because I'm proud of you. I think it's time that we have many legislators who are gay and proud of that fact and do not have to remain in the closet. I think that a gay person, up-front, will not walk away from a responsibility and be afraid of being tossed out of office. After Dade County, I walked among the angry and the frustrated night after night and I looked at their faces. And in San Francisco, three

OPPOSITE: Human billboard during Harvey Milk's second campaign for supervisor, including (left to right) Harry Britt, Carl Carlson, and Harvey Milk, October 1975. FOLLOWING PAGES: Human billboard during Harvey Milk's second campaign for supervisor, including (right to left) Jim Rivaldo, Denton Smith, unknown, unknown, Guy Corry, unknown, Wayne Smolen, unknown, Carl Carlson, Scott Smith, and Harry Britt, October 1975.

days before Gay Pride Day, a person was killed just because he was gay. And that night, I walked among the sad and the frustrated at City Hall in San Francisco and later that night as they lit candles on Castro Street and stood in silence, reaching out for some symbolic thing that would give them hope. These were strong people, people whose faces I knew from the shop, the streets, meetings, and people who I never saw before but I knew. They were strong, but even they needed hope.

And the young gay people in the Altoona, Pennsylvanias, and the Richmond, Minnesotas, who are coming out and hear Anita Bryant on television and her story. The only thing they have to look forward to is hope. And you have to give them hope. Hope for a better world, hope for a better tomorrow, hope for a better place to come to if the pressures at home are too great. Hope that all will be all right. Without hope, not only gays, but the blacks, the seniors, the handicapped, the "us"es, the "us"es will give up. And if you help elect to the central committee and other offices more gay people, that gives a green light to all who feel disenfranchised, a green light to move forward. It means hope to a nation that has given up, because if a gay person makes it, the doors are open to everyone.

So if there is a message I have to give, it is that if I've found one overriding thing about my personal election, it's the fact that if a gay person can be elected, it's a green light. And you and you and you, you have to give people hope. Thank you very much.

— Transcript from the recorded keynote address to the gay caucus of the California Democratic Council on March 10, 1978, in San Diego

Election Day

The morning started just the way I started every morning. The human billboard was out there. I was in the campaign headquarters making sure that everything was together. It was like the lull before the storm. As soon as the polls closed people started coming into campaign headquarters. And before the results were in there were hundreds of people spilling out into the streets.

I was going to go home and get changed after the crazy day, but once things started to pick up there was no way I could leave. I was so hot and sweaty from the crazy day I just pulled out this t-shirt I found there and it was some queen's white t-shirt with the word "HOT" written on it in red sequins, so I put that on—and I was hot, very, very hot. It was that night that Harvey, without warning, just announced, "Anne Kronenberg and Dick Pabich are coming with me to City Hall," and we were just wowed. It was so incredible.

—*Anne Kronenberg*

BELOW: Campaign victory night at Castro Camera, including (left to right) Harry Britt, Wayne Friday, David Weissman, and Bill Krause. OPPOSITE: Joyce Garay (left) and Anne Kronenberg on campaign victory night at Castro Camera, November 8, 1977. FOLLOWING PAGES: Harvey greets the overflow crowd on victory night at Castro Camera, November 8, 1977.

What really counts is does a person care, does a person care about his city or her city? Is a person sensitive to the needs of people and that's the only thing that counts. And that's what San Francisco is saying once again. —*Harvey Milk to an NBC reporter on being elected Supervisor*

This is not my victory—it's yours. If a gay man can win, it proves that there is hope for all minorities who are willing to fight.

—*Harvey Milk*

OPPOSITE: Jack Lira and Harvey Milk at the election night victory party at Castro Camera, November 8, 1977. ABOVE: Sheriff Richard Hongisto, Harvey Milk, and Joyce Garay arriving at Castro Camera to cheers from an ebullient crowd on the night of Harvey's victory. RIGHT: Anne Kronenberg and Harvey Milk onstage at Castro Camera at the election victory party.

Part of the Machine

Our Board of Supervisors, which had always been all white, all male, suddenly had a Chinese person (Gordon Lau), an African American woman (Ella Hill Hutch), a homosexual (Harvey Milk), an unwed mother (Carol Ruth Silver), and a disaffected working-class guy (Dan White). It began to reflect the city, and the city was divided. Everything from the new board came down to a 6/5 vote. —*Cleve Jones*

Harvey became good friends with Gordon Lau, the Chinese Supervisor, particularly after Harvey voted for him over Dianne for board president and they had a joking relationship. Gordon would say, "Harvey, my office needs a little sprucing up, can you send one of your boys over." And Harvey'd shoot back, "I'll take care of redecorating if you'll do my laundry." —*Jim Rivaldo*

This will be the first time in many years that we've seen so many relatively new faces on the San Francisco board of supervisors, and this is probably because it's the first time

in a long time that supervisors have been elected by district instead of citywide. Harvey Milk, a homosexual, the first avowed women's rights advocate, Carol Ruth Silver, the first Chinese American, attorney Gordon Lau, the first black woman, Ella Hill Hutch, and Dan White, a city fireman who gave up his job to take his seat. After the formal swearing-in ceremony, the board elected Dianne Feinstein to be its new president. In a 6 to 5 vote, Feinstein beat Gordon Lau. But then we got the first taste of the new politics. When someone suggested the board vote again to make

it unanimous for Feinstein, newcomers Milk and Silver refused. They stuck to their votes for Lau, to cheers from their supporters. And just about everyone at City Hall was agreeing on one thing—they may be a lot of things, but they probably won't be dull."

—*Jeannine Yeomans, KRON 4*

OPPOSITE: Judge Ollie Marie Victoire and Supervisor Harvey Milk at Milk's inauguration on the steps of San Francisco City Hall, January 9, 1978. ABOVE: Official City Hall portrait of the newly elected San Francisco Board of Supervisors, 1978.

ABOVE: (left to right) Newly elected Supervisor Harvey Milk, Mayor George Moscone, and Supervisor Carol Ruth Silver walking the runway to thunderous applause at the 1978 Empress Coronation, a large-scale drag ball, held as an annual fundraiser by the Tavern Guild, January 28, 1978.

Harvey grew in office. He became interested in other issues as a supervisor. That's the mark of a good politician, to grow in office. He didn't stay where he came in. And I told him once I thought he could be the mayor of San Francisco inside of ten years. He had that kind of potential. —Art Agnos

Harvey always told me to wear my tightest jeans when I went into City Hall; to never blend in. So we all wore these really skintight jeans, where you could tell if people were circumcised. It just made them (the old-school politicians) very nervous. —Cleve Jones

LEFT: Supervisor Harvey Milk as Deputy Mayor for a day, March 7, 1978. OPPOSITE: Supervisor Harvey Milk as clown for a day as part of a promotional publicity campaign for Ringling Brothers and Barnum and Bailey Circus, May 21, 1978.

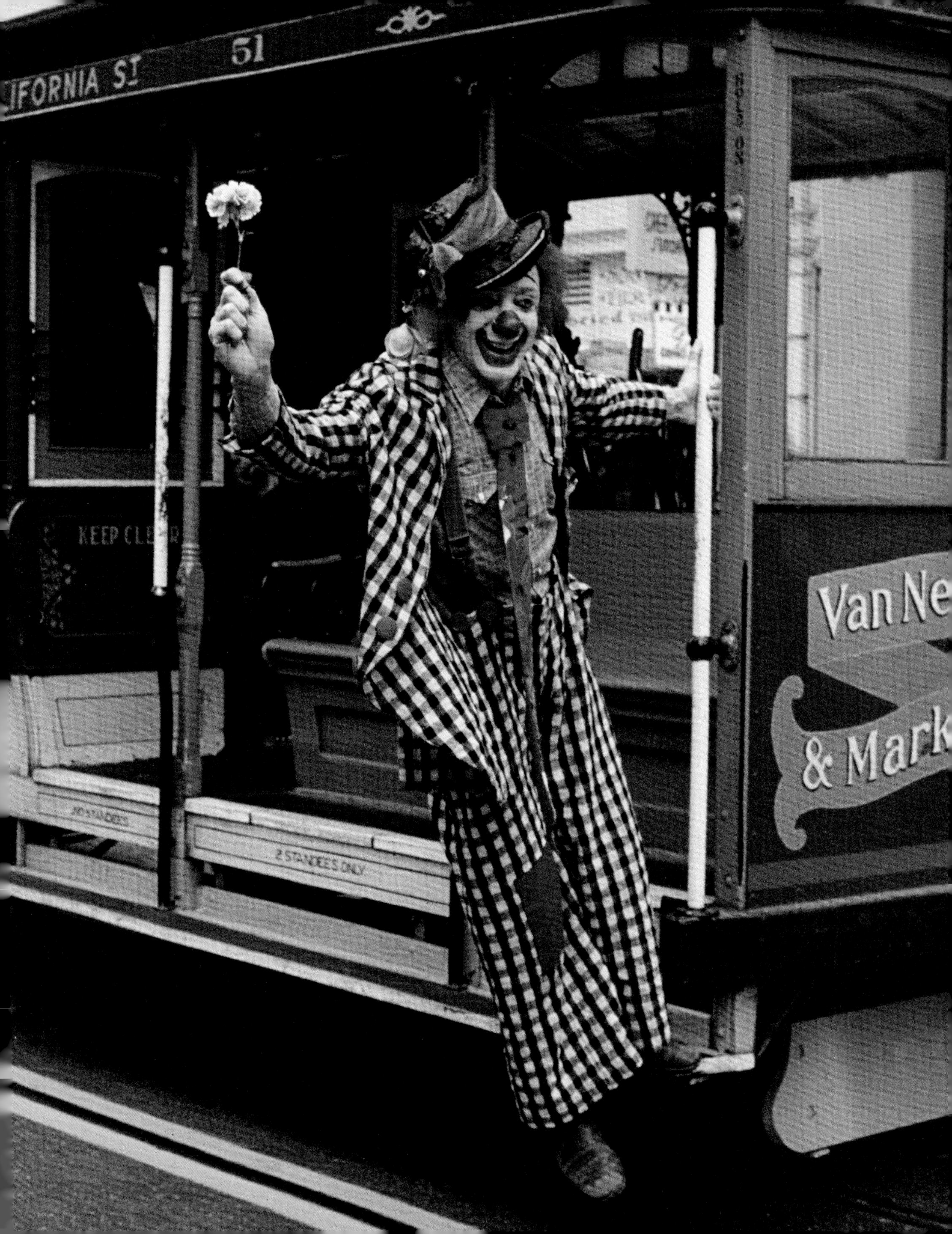
IFORNIA ST
51
HOLD ON
KEEP CLE
Van Ne
& Mark
2 STANDEES ONLY

It's Time for the People

"The people of San Francisco have not labored for years to become prisoners in their own home, locked behind iron gates and bars. I am determined to support and improve the police community efforts being made to stop crime in San Francisco."

Sincerely,
Dan White

"Dan possesses the honesty, integrity and dedication needed to revitalize our community."
Rev. Thomas Lacey

"...and the youth of our parish admire Dan's determination."
Bill Gilheany

"Dan White has the ability to deal decisively with problems which exist in San Francisco today."
Rosemary Farac

Photo/Graphics - STUDIO 7

Dan White for Supervisor
2717 San Bruno Ave.
San Francisco
Mary Ann White; Treasurer

52

"Of the various city workers running for district supervisor, White seems to have put together the best campaign, one that is keyed to his clean cut good looks and obvious sincerity."
Wed., Oct. 5, 1977
S.F. Examiner—Page B-3

Dan White

A DEMOCRATIC CANDIDATE FOR SUPERVISOR

DAN WHITE for SUPERVISOR

Native San Franciscan
Married and living in Excelsior District
Raised in Visitacion Valley
Attended: St. Elizabeth's Grammar School
Riordan High School
Woodrow Wilson High School
City College of San Francisco
United States Army (3 years)
Vietnam Veteran—Sergeant, Paratrooper Corps
Former San Francisco Policeman
At present a San Francisco Fireman

For years we have witnessed an exodus from San Francisco by many of our family members, friends and neighbors. Alarmed by the enormous increase in crime, poor educational facilities and a deteriorating social structure, they have fled to temporary havens through the Bay Area. I reiterate—temporary havens; for the problems that exist (and there are many) do not recognize city or county boundaries.

In a few short years these problems will erupt from our city and engulf the tree lined, sunbathed communities that chide us for "daring" to live in San Francisco. That is, unless we who have remained unite and fight for those values which will strengthen our society.

Individually we are helpless. Yet you must realize there are thousands upon thousands of frustrated, angry people, such as yourselves, anxious to eradicate the problems which blight our beautiful city. Only by banding together with other responsible residents of San Francisco and taking positive action can we accomplish this goal.

It saddens me to witness what has occurred, and unfortunately continues to occur. I am not going to be forced out of San Francisco by splinter groups of radicals and social deviates. Believe me, there are tens of thousands who are just as determined to legally fight to protect and defined our ideals.

By choosing to run for Supervisor, I have committed myself to the confrontation which can no longer be avoided by those who care. Together we can win!!!

Dan White

I'm not going to be forced out of San Francisco by splinter groups of social radicals, social deviants, and incorrigibles. You must realize there are thousands upon thousands of frustrated angry people such as yourselves waiting to unleash a fury that will eradicate the malignancies which blight our beautiful city. —*Dan White*

ABOVE: Dan White at twenty-six, showing off his physique and his new shamrock tattoo. LEFT: Supervisors Harvey Milk and Dan White, circa 1978. OPPOSITE: OPPOSITE: Dan White campaign literature, 1977.

DIED. Dan White, 39, former San Francisco supervisor who in 1978 shot to death the city's mayor, George Moscone, and its first openly homosexual supervisor, Harvey Milk; by his own hand (carbon-monoxide poisoning); in San Francisco. At his 1979 trial, White pleaded "diminished capacity," contending that a diet of sugary junk food had aggravated his severe psychological problems, an argument that became known as the "Twinkie defense." When White was convicted only of voluntary manslaughter, 5,000 rioters, most of them gays, stormed city hall. Following his release after five years in prison, White, unemployed and dogged by fears of retaliation, lived undercover, apart from his family.

—Time *Magazine, Monday April 18, 1985*

The Briggs Initiative: Prop 6

Proposition 6 was the California state-wide ballot initiative that would have authorized the firing of any openly gay teachers or their supporters. Against all odds, Proposition 6 was defeated on November 7, 1978, highlighting Millk's campaign based on the critical importance of "coming out."

Now that I'm older, and now that I've seen what I've seen, he's absolutely right. The single most important thing for any gay person to do, regardless of their circumstances or their politics, or whatever, the single most important political act, as well as personal, spiritual, emotional, is just simply to reveal their true selves. —*Cleve Jones*

I think he really believed that he was the one who could be the most effective in fighting the Briggs initiative. And he was right. To do something on a statewide level. . . it just needed to have somebody like Harvey doing

the campaigning. He recognized that, and he put himself out there as the spokesperson, self-appointed spokesperson. And thank God he did. —*Anne Kronenberg*

We'd had this great victory, an incredibly unexpected victory over Briggs, a resounding victory. We defeated them. It was such a decisive, unexpected, incredible victory, especially for Harvey because he had been our primary spokesperson, along with Sally Gearhart. —*Cleve Jones*

ABOVE: Harvey Milk interviewed by a reporter at the "No on 6" campaign headquarters, November 7, 1978. LEFT: Gay rally, 1978. OPPOSITE: "No on 6" campaign brochure, 1978.

PROP 6 THREATENS EVERYONE.

Proposition 6 has been called the "anti-homosexual teacher initiative."

But this is misleading.

The issues extend far beyond an attempt to ban homosexuals from schools. More people than teachers are directly affected.

Any teacher could be fired for expressing his or her opinions outside the school.

Legal experts agree with a Los Angeles *Times* editorial which states: "A school board employee who spoke out for fair treatment of homosexuals could be fired. Expression of personal beliefs in the course of private life would be enough to warrant dismissal."

A letter-to-the-editor opposing discrimination against homosexuals could be classified as "advocating homosexual conduct."

The writer would be fired—even if he or she were heterosexual.

Proposition 6 requires government prying into private lives.

Teachers could be accused because of unfounded rumors—or just because a student or co-worker disliked them.

STOP BRIGGS

NO ON 6

PROTECT YOUR RIGHTS

BACABI/NO on 6

My name is Harvey Milk, and I want to recruit you. I want to recruit you for the fight to preserve your democracy from the John Briggs and the Anita Bryants who are trying to constitutionalize bigotry. . .

Gay brothers and sisters, what are you going to do about it? You must come out! Come out to your parents. I know that it is hard and will hurt them, but think about how they will hurt you in the voting booth! Come out to your relatives. I know that is hard and will upset them but think of how they will upset you in the voting booth. Come out to your friends if indeed they are your friends. Come out to your neighbors, to your fellow workers, to the people who work where you eat and shop. . .

Once and for all, break down the myths, destroy the lies and distortions. For your sake. For their sake. For the sake of the youngsters who are becoming scared by the votes from Dade to Eugene. . .

—*Harvey Milk*

BELOW: Supervisor Harvey Milk in his last San Francisco Gay and Lesbian Freedom Day Parade, June 25, 1978. OPPOSITE: Supervisor Harvey Milk speaking on the main stage at the San Francisco Gay and Lesbian Freedom Day Parade, June 25, 1978. FOLLOWING PAGES: San Francisco City Hall protest of the press conference by Senator John Briggs announcing Proposition 6, the California state-wide ballot initiative that would have authorized the firing of any openly gay teachers or their supporters, June 1978.

Assassination

On Sunday night, the night before the murders, Harvey went to the opera. He was talking about how great it had been. Harvey was shot in Dan White's little cubicle area and there was a streak of blood going down the wall with Harvey lying on the floor. And out the window all you could see was the opera house.   —*Jim Rivaldo*

I saw Harvey's feet sticking out Dan White's office door. And I knew it was Harvey because Harvey only had one pair of shoes. He had one old battered pair of wingtips that had holes in the bottoms and I recognized them. . . and

they turned his body over. . . and that was the first time I ever saw a dead person. Then it's all sort of a blur."   —*Cleve Jones*

He was dad to me. You know, my father and I have become very close since, but at that point we weren't really getting along very well. I felt despair, like everything's gone. I just kept saying that over to myself, you know, it's all over now. It's over. We'd lost everything.   — *Cleve Jones*

OPPOSITE: After the Candlelight March, people placing their candles in memory of Mayor George Moscone and Supervisor Harvey Milk on the statue of Lincoln at San Francisco City Hall, November 27, 1978

OPPOSITE: Candlelight March with thirty to forty thousand marching in silence that night in honor of Mayor George Moscone and Supervisor Harvey Milk, November 27, 1978. ABOVE: The bodies of Mayor George Moscone and Supervisor Harvey Milk lying in state in San Francisco City Hall Rotunda, December 1978.

White Night Riots

A reporter called me from the Hall of Justice crying. She could hardly speak. "He got off, he got off, they gave him manslaughter. Five years, five years, can you believe it?" My first reaction was to vomit. —*Cleve Jones*

The Civic Center was full, a line of police cars exploding on McAllister, people storming the front of City Hall, fires in the basement, all the windows shattered. Then the police made the gladiator line and just swept through. And when faced with a line of helmets, with shielded cops beating their armor, the crowd just panicked. Tens of thousands of people just started running, screaming through Civic Center Plaza. Tear gas, smoke, explosions, sirens, absolute chaos. This was because we lost Harvey, and Dan White got off on manslaughter. In the midst of all the chaos I thought we had to fight back. We cannot be trampled like this. I got a couple other people and we just started chanting "slow down . . . don't run . . . slow down . . . don't run." The chant caught on and the crowd slowed and stopped running. The cops who'd been chasing us had fallen out of formation and were no longer a unified front, shield to shield, baton to baton. Soon thousands of people in the plaza were chanting, "don't run, turn around, fight back, don't run!" At this electric moment 15,000 people who had been running away turned on their heels and charged back into the police line, hurling themselves on the cops, ripping parking meters out of the concrete, kicking in police windows, blowing up police cars. —*Cleve Jones*

OPPOSITE and FOLLOWING PAGES: White Night Riots— demonstrations and rioting on the night of the announcement of the penalty phase of the Dan White verdict, May 21, 1979

Part 2

MILK

The Making of the Movie

This is Harvey Milk speaking on Friday, November 18th. This is to be played only in the event of my death by assassination . . .

In His Own Write

Every movement needs a hero. As the years pass and the change that hero fought for has been effected, it is common to forget just how much one person made a difference.

Milk screenwriter Dustin Lance Black first heard about Harvey Milk while working in theater in the early 1990s. A few years later, Black watched the Academy Award–winning 1984 documentary feature *The Times of Harvey Milk*. He remembers, "Harvey Milk is giving a speech at the end and he essentially says, 'Somewhere in Des Moines or San Antonio'—which is where I'm from—'there's a young gay person who might open a paper, and it says "Homosexual elected in San Francisco" and know that there's hope for a better world, there's hope for a better tomorrow.'

"I just broke down crying because I was very much that kid and he was giving me hope. He was saying, not only are you okay but you can do great things. And that's the moment I thought, we have to get that story back out there, we've got to continue the message."

A few years later, Black had gained a foothold in film and television, working as a writer, producer, and director. He felt that he could tell

OPPOSITE: Sean Penn as Harvey Milk. RIGHT: Harvey Milk at Castro Camera, circa 1977.

the story of the man who has been called "the gay MLK [Martin Luther King Jr.]." However, he notes, "I didn't have the rights to a book [on Milk, of which there are several], so I started to do research on my own. Several industry folks told me to forget about it, that it was too risky. But my credit card and I pressed on."

Although a quarter-century had passed, he was glad to discover that many of the people who were close to Milk and had been instrumental in his efforts were still alive. Black notes, "My

113

strategy from the beginning had been to make use of firsthand accounts and stories. I wanted to find out the details for myself rather than reading it somewhere else, I wanted things a writer can't get out of a book or an article." The first person Black met with was Cleve Jones, one of Milk's protégés and among his closest confidants.

"Boy, is Cleve a gift for a writer," Black says. "I initially interviewed him over two days and filled eight hours' worth of little cassette tapes."

Jones introduced him to—among others— Danny Nicoletta, Anne Kronenberg, Allan Baird, Carol Ruth Silver, Frank Robinson, Tom Ammiano, Jim Rivaldo, Art Agnos, and Michael Wong.

Black admits, "It took a lot to convince some of Harvey's real-life contemporaries that I was someone who could make this thing happen and that they weren't wasting their time. I made assurances, but I myself wasn't really sure I could pull it off. Some of them became like family to me and confided some painful memories, and I was terrified of letting them down."

ABOVE: Screenwriter Dustin Lance Black (right) with director Gus Van Sant on set. OPPOSITE: Sean Penn as Harvey Milk with James Franco as Scott Smith.

Black concentrated on which relationships were key to Milk and which ones were representative of the movement. As was so often the case with Milk, the two would converge.

"Harvey was personally connected to why he was doing what he did. It wasn't just about rights or electoral politics, it was about the fact that he was in love with Scott or he was in love with Jack Lira, and he wanted that to be okay. He wanted to have the right to be himself, because when he was a young man, and even when he first came to San Francisco, it was against the law to be in a gay relationship, to dance with a man, or to be in a gay bar. His is an intensely personal story, even when it is a political one. As a screenwriter, this was one of those rare chances to tell a story where the two are absolutely connected. It was politics for the sake of love."

The Direct Approach(es)

To put Harvey Milk into cinematic narrative terms, Dustin Lance Black went through numerous screenplay drafts over a nearly four-year period. "I gave up a lot of nights and weekends," he remembers. "During the week, it was *Big Love* until 6 or 7 at night, then *Milk* from 7 to midnight."

"I thought Lance's script was beautiful," Cleve Jones says. "It had a very simple, elegant structure. Harvey's voice was clear in it; I could hear Harvey saying the words Lance had written. And I told Lance that when he was ready, I had a director for the project."

Black says, "When Cleve told me his friend who wanted to direct was Gus Van Sant, I said, 'Oh, that's good!'"

Van Sant reflects, "*The Times of Harvey Milk* documentary had set the bar pretty high, but I felt a dramatic version would be an important continuation of the story. There would always be difficulty in telling it because of the many elements of Harvey's life and the many other intersecting stories at Castro Camera, but Lance got it in line and wrote a succinct script that was largely about the politics and less about the day-to-day lives of the characters.

"Harvey Milk is one of the more illustrious gay activists, and since he died in the line of duty, he has achieved sainthood in the gay world. One reason to make this film was for younger people who weren't around during his time; to remember him, and to learn about him."

Black was friends with the producing team of Dan Jinks and Bruce Cohen, Academy Award winners for *American Beauty*. Both knew of Milk when they were growing up; Jinks' father had been editor of *The San Jose Mercury-News*, which followed Milk's campaigns and triumphs.

Jinks notes, "I read that Lance had written a screenplay about Harvey Milk and that Gus Van Sant would be directing, so I called to congratulate him and he said, 'You know, we don't have a producer. Would you be interested in reading this?' I said, 'Are you kidding? Absolutely!'"

Cohen adds, "We felt that the film could be both moving and entertaining. This man was not your average politician; he came out to San Francisco with Scott Smith with the goal of

OPPOSITE: Castro Camera, circa 1973, and below the re-creation of the image in the film. ABOVE: First assistant director David Webb and Gus Van Sant.

expressing himself and living his life and being out and creating this new world for himself. He didn't plan to go into politics, but he felt he could make a difference."

Jinks remarks, "One of the benchmarks of the script is authenticity, thanks to Lance's research. The script tells Harvey's heroic story so powerfully, but also hilariously, and sexily. Combine that with the confirmed involvement of a world-class filmmaker, and we immediately said, 'We have to be a part of this.'"

As for talent, Sean Penn leapt to the forefront of everyone's minds as the project coalesced. Cohen notes, "He has this way of just inhabiting a character so you couldn't find the actor underneath if you tried." Van Sant knew the Oscar-winning actor— who now lives in the Bay Area—and sent the script to him. Penn responded even quicker to the script than Van Sant had, and within a week, Black and Van Sant were meeting with him. Penn wanted assurances that the filmmaking team would be as authentic with Milk's personal relationships as they were with his politics.

Black admits, "We were mindful of whether a lead actor would take risks. But Sean said, 'Let's do it right. Let's tell it like it is.' He is dedicated to

so intriguing. I felt honored to be a part of this movie and to be playing an extraordinary man like George Moscone. He believed in freedom and civil rights for all. Hopefully, *Milk* will awaken the need for people to do something against intolerance and bigotry."

Kelvin Yu, cast as Milk's close advisor Michael Wong, spent time with the man he would be portraying but also availed himself of the journal that had been such a help to Black. The actor reports, "It's 370 pages, all in first person, and Michael's bullshit meter is perfect. In Harvey, he saw somebody who was the real thing.

"Michael was a rebel but he did it in ways that are more substantial and less cosmetic than what people think being a rebel is like. He was deter-

OPPOSITE: Supervisor Harvey Milk with Jack Lira and supporters on the inauguration walk from the Castro neighborhood to San Francisco City Hall, January 9, 1978. ABOVE: Sean Penn and Diego Luna re-create the scene.

mined to use the political system to fight for civil rights, with voting and through democracy."

Wong states simply, "I hope the film will show that you can be an ordinary person who happens to be gay and can do something extraordinary like Harvey Milk did."

Rolling

Dustin Lance Black muses, "On the first day of shooting I finally breathed a sigh of relief. Something I started four years earlier was coming to fruition. We did it; it was really happening. I started crying when we saw that rainbow that first day. Cleve Jones had tears in his eyes, too."

Jones elaborates, "It was the worst possible morning, drenching and cold. Two minutes before the cameras were to start rolling, the clouds parted, the sun came out and this enormous rainbow appeared over the set. A sign, I thought."

Gus Van Sant and his frequent cinematographer Harris Savides were unfazed by weather

concerns. Embarking on their fifth movie together, Van Sant notes, "Every picture that Harris and I have done has been a journey in terms of figuring out how we'll film it. For *Milk,* we knew it would be different than the smaller films we've made." Despite the larger scale, the director and cinematographer did not use storyboards but followed their collaborative and exploratory approach.

Van Sant adds, "We start out knowing that the possibilities are endless, then we pare them down to the most interesting ones. Sometimes we reference films or photos, but we consider everything to end up with a handful of ideas we like."

On the set, Black reports, "I learned so much from watching Gus. His style is different than any other director I've worked with—it's very organic; he steps back and understands how to let things happen and finds the unexpected. He allows the actors and artists around him to discover things."

Alison Pill enthuses, "It's sort of flying by the seat of your pants with the huge element of trust.

It's inspiring because you have to be present in every single moment."

Emile Hirsch offers, "Gus makes you use your legs as an actor instead of being a crutch. That pushes his actors to be brave and trust their instincts. He is extraordinary to work with."

On Location

Milk was filmed entirely on location in San Francisco, with a home base at Treasure Island. For the filmmakers it couldn't have been done anywhere else. "The spirit and energy of this film *is* San Francisco," Dustin Lance Black says. Bruce Cohen adds, "All of us felt from the very beginning that San Francisco was a character in the story. The story changed the city forever, and is woven into its history and its fabric.

"We went looking for a place to re-create Castro Camera, and ended up going to the exact location where it was at 575 Castro Street. We went

it was because that business was open in the year the scene was taking place."

Costume designer Danny Glicker and his staff made copious use of the various collections of photographs. Glicker notes, "From a strictly visual standpoint, my guardian angel was Danny Nicoletta. In the 1970s, San Francisco was the place where cultural change was exploding and constantly evolving. As a costume designer, this was an enormously appealing challenge. It was important to be detail-driven as opposed to having a grandiose concept.

"I love old clothes and whenever possible will use the real thing. Getting skin-tight jeans for everyone was a huge challenge because bodies have evolved since. I went to some serious dumps looking for jeans, sometimes paying large amounts for beautifully broken-in Levi's from the '70s!

"One of the first things Cleve Jones told me is that Harvey always had the same few items of clothing on. When he needed something for his political career he went to secondhand stores. His shoes had holes in them, and when he was being carried out of his office after being assassinated, Cleve saw the holes and knew it was Harvey. We had an entire binder on Harvey. Based on the research, if a scene corresponded with an actual outfit, we labeled it so."

The other actors were sparked by their research, too. Glicker says, "Some of them wore items from the real people they were portraying. Alison Pill had an earring that Anne Kronenberg

OPPOSITE: Supervisor Harvey Milk in his last
San Francisco Gay and Lesbian Freedom Day Parade,
June 25, 1978

wore every day back then; Lucas Grabeel wore one of Danny Nicoletta's vests; and, perhaps most touchingly, George Moscone's son Jonathan brought one of his father's ties to the set for Victor Garber to wear when the mayor swears Harvey in as supervisor."

Today's San Franciscans found part of their city going back in time for weeks on end. Rainbow Flags had to be removed or covered up because much of the film takes place prior to its 1978 un-veiling. Favorite hot spots like Aquarius Records, China Court, and Toad Hall reappeared, stories were told, memories were exchanged, and the ex-citement of a time of change and realized potential was palpably recalled. Harvey Milk was bringing people together again.

On February 8, 2008, the re-creation of the candlelight vigil—uniting tens of thousands of San Franciscans of all ages, races, and sexual orienta-tions as they struggled to cope with the shock and grief of the murders—was filmed.

The production was able to engage several thousand extras—including many who had marched in 1978—and, as they had 30 years prior, Cleve Jones and Gilbert Baker were among those putting out calls for San Franciscans to participate.

Executive producer Michael London says, "It was as if the city had stopped again 30 years later. There was an outpouring of people. From the moment they started walking and the cameras started rolling, you felt the loss."

Gus Van Sant marvels, "It was wonderful to have the help of so many San Franciscans. They really got into it and were an enormous help. Thank you, San Francisco."

Milk's Legacy

The cumulative effects of Harvey Milk's break-throughs remain in the culture and politics of today. The gay rights movement has come a long way, but the pendulum continues to swing.

Some countries (Canada, Spain, Denmark) have legalized same-sex marriages. Some American states like California have followed suit only to take the right away again (with the passage of Prop 8 on November 4, 2008).

OPPOSITE: Josh Brolin as Dan White with Sean Penn as Harvey Milk

Bruce Cohen remarks, "Harvey Milk's story shows what one man can accomplish, but it also reminds us how far we still have to go."

Dustin Lance Black adds, "For me, Harvey's greatest legacy is that his story of hope has saved, and will continue to save, lives. I consider myself to be one of them. There are still kids out there who are coming out, and who need to know that there are gay heroes and gay icons."

Cleve Jones states, "It is important for us to know our history and to learn from it. I am some-times fearful that the generations are unaware of how many people had to struggle so long and so hard to have the beginning of freedom that we have now. History is full of examples of people who thought they were free, thought they were secure, but found out overnight that they were living in a fool's paradise. We are winning, yet all this could be taken away in the blink of an eye." ▼

Timeline

Acknowledgments

We would like to extend our thanks to the following people for their editorial assistance and contributions: to Art Agnos, Allan Baird, Cleve Jones, Anne Kronenberg, Jim Rivaldo, and Michael Wong for their perceptive insights; to Armistead Maupin for opening the book with his lively memories of Harvey Milk; to photographer Dan Nicoletta who was invaluable helping us collect the fascinating photos; to photographers Phil Bray, Donald Eckert, Rink Foto, Jerry Pritikin, and Efren Ramirez; to Christina Moretta and Susan Goldstein at the San Francisco Public Library; to Rebekah Kim at the GLBT Historical Society; to *Milk* production designer Bill Groom; to Jason Simos and James Ferrera for their production notes; to book designer Timothy Shaner and editor Christopher Measom at Night and Day Design; and to Newmarket Editorial Project Director Keith Hollaman.

We are also grateful for the cooperation and support of producers Bruce Cohen, Dan Jinks, Michael London, and Bill Horberg; and especially of the Focus Features team, including James Schamus, David Brooks, Adriene Bowles, Harlan Gulko, Meg Greengold, David Bloch, and Sasha Silver.

Most of all, thanks to Gus Van Sant for the brilliant film and to screenwriter Dustin Lance Black for his stirring introduction and wonderful guidance in shaping this book. —*Esther Margolis, Publisher, Newmarket Press*

Permissions

Permission to reprint copyrighted material from the following sources is gratefully acknowledged. The publisher has made all reasonable efforts to contact copyright holders for permission; any errors in the form of credit given will be corrected in future printings.

Dan Nicoletta: Pages 6, 9, 10, 19, 30, 31, 32-33, 34, 35, 39, 41, 48, 51, 52, 53, 59, 64, 66, 67, 70, 76, 80, 81, 82-83, 88-89, 94, 98, 100, 101, 107, 108-109, 113, 128. Copyright © by Dan Nicoletta. All rights reserved. **Harvey Milk Archives – Scott Smith Collection, Gay & Lesbian Center, San Francisco Public Library**: Pages 1, 16, 22, 23, 24, 25 (both photos), 26 (all 3 photos), 27, 28, 38 (photo by Rink Foto), 40 (both photos), 42 (both photos), 43, 44 (top photo), 56-57, 65, 72 (photo probably by Scott Smith), 78-79 (photo by Leland Toy), 92 (both photos), 116 (top photo) (probably by Harvey Milk or Scott Smith). **San Francisco History Center, San Francisco Public Library:** Page 87, 90. **Gay, Lesbian, Bisexual, Transgender Historical Society:** Pages 36-37 (photo by Maria Ueda), 54 (photo by Crawford Barton), 55 (photo by Crawford Barton), 84 (photo by Crawford Barton), 95 (photo by Maria Ueda), 103 (photo by Crawford Barton), 105 (photo by Crawford Barton). **Bill Acheson:** Page 60. **Crawford Barton:** Pages 54, 55, 84, 103, 105. **Marc Cohen:** Page 46. Courtesy of Dan Nicoletta. **Ann Creighton:** Page 85. **Dennis DeSilva:** Page 91 (both photos). Copyright © by Dennis DeSilva. All rights reserved. **Donald Eckert:** Pages 13, 68-69, 135. Copyright © by Donald Eckert. All rights reserved. Website: Uncle Donald's Castro Street (http://thecastro.net). **Rink Foto:** Pages 38, 58, 71. Copyright © by Rink Foto 1978. All rights reserved. **Armistead Maupin:** Page 8. Courtesy of Armistead Maupin. **Harvey Milk:** Pages 40 (lower left photo), 47. Courtesy of Dan Nicoletta. **Jerry Pritikin:** Pages 62 ("Save Our Rights—Orange Tuesday 6/7/77") and 63 ("Bigots on Parade—1977 San Francisco Gay Day Parade"). Copyright © by Jerry Pritikin/Chicago. All rights reserved. **Efren Ramirez** Pages 44, 75, 86, 96-97, 133. Copyright © by Efren Ramirez. All rights reserved. *San Francisco Examiner:* Page 98. Used by permission of San Francisco Examiner. **Denton Smith:** Page 49. Courtesy of Dan Nicoletta. **Scott Smith:** Page 72. **Leland Toy**: Pages 78-79. **Maria Ueda:** Pages 36-37, 95. **David Waggoner:** Page 121. Courtesy of Dan Nicoletta. **All unit photography from the movie *Milk* by Dan Nicoletta and Phil Bray.** Unit photography and movie stills from *Milk* © 2008 Focus Features LLC and Axon Film Finance I, LLC. All rights reserved. Pages 112, 114, 115, 116, 117, 118-119, 122, 123, 124-125, 126, 127, 129, 130, 131, 132, 134, 136, 137, 138-139. **Page 121:** Photo on left by Scott Green. **Page 123**: Middle photo by Tom DeSanto/Courtesy of Brandon Boyce.

Permission for use of text extracts is acknowledged from the following sources:

Page 63: Miami, May 9—"A dispute over rights..." by B. Drummond Ayres, Jr., excerpted from *The New York Times*, May 10, 1977. Used by permission of *The New York Times*. **Pages 72-77:** Hope Speech: Courtesy of Harvey Milk Archives – Scott Smith Collection, Gay & Lesbian Center, San Francisco Public Library. Copyright © 1978 by Estate of Harvey Milk. All rights reserved. **Page 91:** Dan White "Milestone" from *Time* Magazine, April 18, 1985. Copyright © 1985, Time Inc. All rights reserved. Reprinted by permission. **Pages 102-105:** "Harvey Milk—The Pioneer" by John Cloud, from *Time* Magazine, June 14, 1999. Copyright © 1999, Time Inc. All rights reserved. Reprinted by permission.

Quotes from Dustin Lance Black's interviews from research for the movie *Milk* appear on pages 29, 35, 42, 44, 49, 50, 52, 53, 57, 59, 61, 65, 66, 66, 80, 86, 88, 92, 98, 106. Used by kind permission of Art Agnos, Cleve Jones, Anne Kronenberg, Jim Rivaldo, and Michael Wong.